GAS

Wayne Jackman

Consultants: British Gas plc

Wayland

Titles in this series

Bricks	Paper
Electricity	Plastics
Gas	Steel
Glass	Water
Oil	Wood

Cover: (Main picture) Drilling for gas at sea. (Top right) In the last thirty years, natural gas has become a popular source of fuel.

Series editor: Sarah Doughty
Book editor: Paul Bennett

First published in 1992 by
Wayland (Publishers) Ltd
61 Western Road, Hove
East Sussex BN3 1JD, England

British Library Cataloguing in Publication Data
Jackman, Wayne
  Gas. – (Links Series)
  I. Title   II. Series
  665.7

ISBN 0 7502 0616 0

Typeset by Dorchester Typesetting Group Ltd
Printed in Italy by G. Canale & C.S.p.A.
Bound in Belgium by Casterman S.A.

Contents

All the words that appear in
bold are explained in
the glossary on page 30.

How gas was formed

Many millions of years ago, even before the dinosaurs roamed the earth, much of the land was covered in thick jungle and swamp. The seas swarmed with tiny creatures called **plankton**.

When the jungle plants and plankton died, they sank to the bottom of the swamps or to the sea-bed. As they rotted, they were covered with layers of sand and mud which began to squash them. As more plants and plankton died, they were also covered by sand and mud. Each new layer squashed the others below it.

Gas was formed millions of years ago in swamps like this .

Over millions of years, the mud and sand became harder, and their weight changed the dead plants and plankton into gas and tiny drops of **crude oil**.

Sometimes the leaves of the plants or the bodies of the creatures turned into stone. These are called fossils. Coal, oil and gas are all called fossil fuels because they were formed from living things which died millions of years ago.

__Below left__ This diagram shows how the sand and mud layers built up, squashing the dead plankton and turning them into gas.

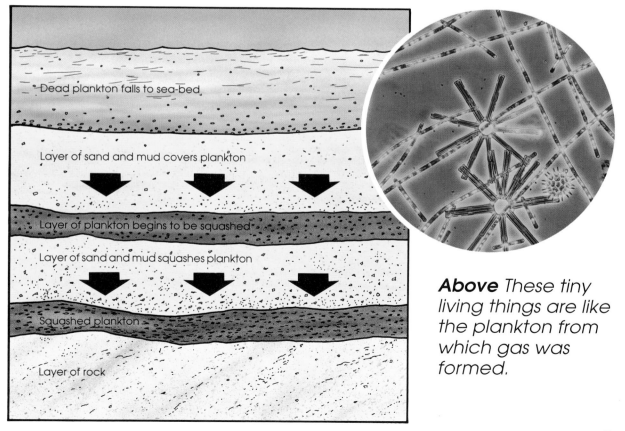

Dead plankton falls to sea-bed

Layer of sand and mud covers plankton

Layer of plankton begins to be squashed

Layer of sand and mud squashes plankton

Squashed plankton

Layer of rock

__Above__ These tiny living things are like the plankton from which gas was formed.

Exploring for gas

Gas is very light, and so it tries to seep upwards through the layers of rock which have been formed from mud and sand. If a layer of rock has tiny holes in it, then the gas can pass through. These holes are called pores. If the gas meets a layer of rock without these pores, such as clay, then it becomes trapped.

Geologists can find gas on land or at sea by listening to shock waves from explosions.

Geologists have the difficult job of finding the trapped gas. They send sound waves down through the layers of rock, which bounce

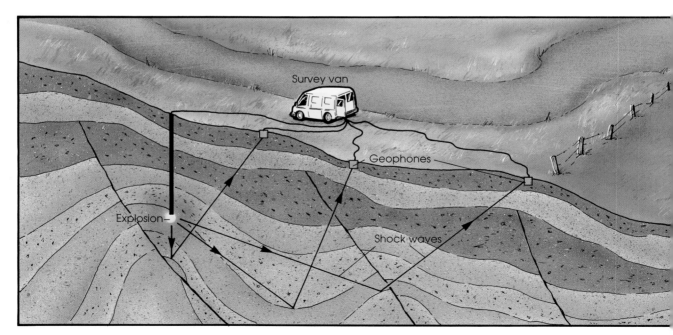

Survey van

Geophones

Explosion

Shock waves

back rather like an echo. By recording the 'echoes', the geologists build up a detailed picture of the structure of the rock below the surface. They can also listen to the shock waves from small explosions that they set off in the ground, or use photographs from space **satellites**. A special helicopter can even 'sniff' the air to see if any gas is being released from the rock below.

From all this information, geologists are able to find out where gas *might* be trapped. But the only way to be sure is to dig an **exploratory well**.

Above The result of a geological survey is carefully studied. The black lines on the chart represent shock waves.

Survey ship

Geophones   Floating cable

Shot fired

Shock waves

Drilling for gas

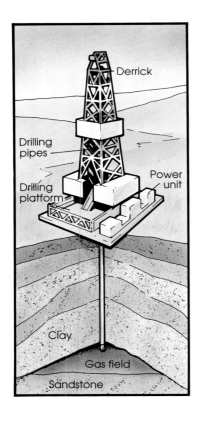

When a likely location of trapped gas is found, the exploratory well is drilled. A **drilling rig** bores a hole down into the rock to a depth of about 3,000 m.

Gas is very often found together with oil, but not always. An area rich in just gas is called a gas field. If gas is discovered, then several more bore holes are drilled around the area to find out if there is enough gas to make **production** worthwhile. If there is, then a permanent drilling

Above A drilling rig is built once gas has been discovered.

Right Gas is often discovered in places that are hard to get to. This drilling rig is in the middle of a forest.

structure called a Christmas tree is built. This is an arrangement of valves, pipes and gauges with a tall tower in the centre called a derrick.

The derrick holds the drill and all the pipes that are fed into the ground to bring out the gas. The workers who join the pipes together are called roughnecks.

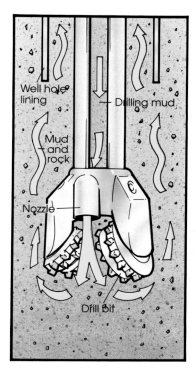

Above *The drill bit has sharp teeth to cut its way through the rock.*

Left *A roughneck stands by a new drill bit.*

Gas under the sea

Huge reserves of gas and oil lie under the sea and so are difficult to reach.

Giant jack-up rigs or semi-submersible rigs are used to drill an exploratory well. Jack-up rigs are towed into position and held in place by lowering long legs, which then rest on the sea-bed. Semi-submersible rigs float in the water and are kept in position with the help of a computer.

A semi-submersible rig is transported to its position by a carrier ship.

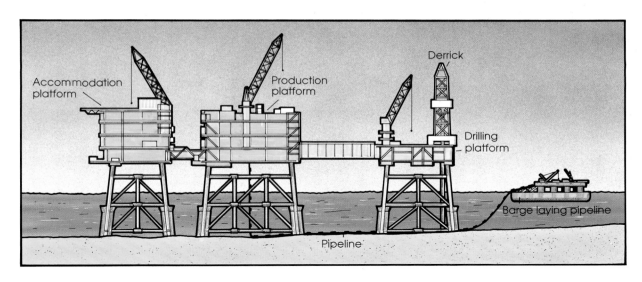

Accommodation platform

Production platform

Derrick

Drilling platform

Barge laying pipeline

Pipeline

When large amounts of gas are found, a production platform is built to pipe it up. Often gas is found hundreds of kilometres from land. This means that long pipelines have to be laid on the sea-bed to pipe it ashore. So, you can see that **offshore** drilling is a very complicated business!

This diagram shows just how large and complicated a drilling rig at sea has to be.

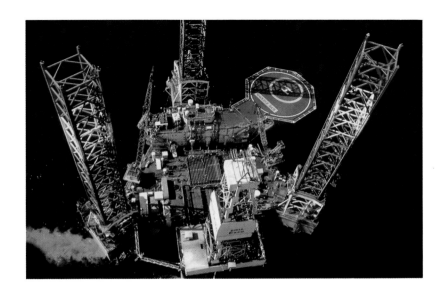

A jack-up rig seen from a helicopter.

Refining and storing gas

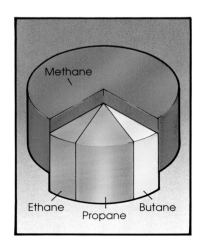

The different gases that make up natural gas.

Natural gas consists mainly of methane, but contains small amounts of other gases. These are butane, propane and ethane.

Before the gas is pumped into the supply pipelines, it is cleaned. Water and **impurities** are taken out and the smell people recognize as gas is added. This is a safety precaution, so that people will know when gas is leaking.

Large amounts of gas are kept in storage so a lot of people can use it all at the same time.

This gas terminal in Yorkshire, Britain, is about the size of a small town.

Storage tanks at a gas refinery in Mexico.

Gas holders in towns and cities can hold enough for the people who live there. But there are a number of other ways of storing natural gas. It can be frozen to −160°C. At this temperature it becomes **liquid natural gas (LNG)**, and can be stored in tanks.

Other gases that are part of natural gas are also turned into liquids. These are called **liquid petroleum gases (LPGs)** and are stored in **cylinders** or tanks.

13

Transporting gas

Gas fields and gas **refineries** can be a long way from where the gas is actually needed. To transport it to homes and factories, large underground pipelines are used. Sometimes the pipelines cross several countries. The trans-Siberian pipeline is 6,000 km long!

Another way of transporting gas is to use **refrigerated** carrier ships. These carry LNG to countries that do not have their own supplies of gas, such as Japan.

Above *This unusual-looking ship is transporting LNG in refrigerated tanks.*

Right *A giant underground pipeline is being laid to carry gas from a refinery to towns and cities.*

Once the gas reaches towns and cities, it passes into the local **distribution system**, which is made up of smaller pipes. These travel under our streets and into houses and factories. Nowadays, these pipes are made from very tough plastics, which can withstand the shaking from passing traffic. They need to be strong and last a long time, because digging up the roads to repair the pipes is expensive and very inconvenient.

Towns have a network of underground pipes to deliver gas to the houses and factories.

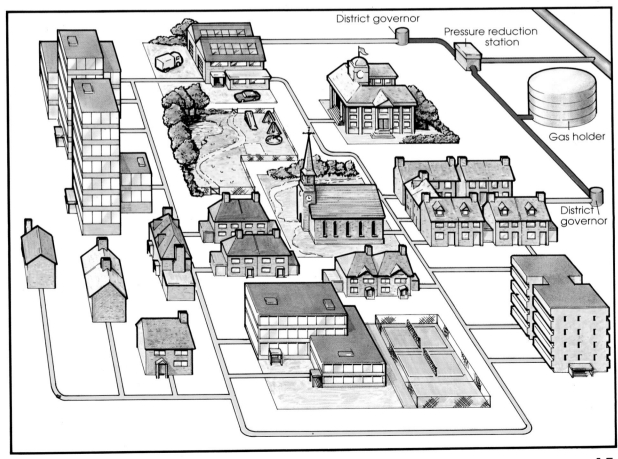

District governor

Pressure reduction station

Gas holder

District governor

How gas is used

Many swimming pools are heated by gas.

In the last century, gas was made from coal. The gas was used for lighting homes and streets. However, when electricity was supplied to homes and industry, this gas became used less and less. But the development of large supplies of natural gas in the last thirty years once again made gas a popular source of fuel.

Natural gas is relatively cheap, easily available and produces few poisonous fumes. For these reasons, it is used in many different countries.

A gas fire heats a room quickly.

In the home, it is used to cook meals, to heat water and to run **central heating** systems. Fridges can run on gas and so can tumble driers! It is also used to heat schools, hospitals, swimming pools, shops and offices.

In factories, gas is used to heat ovens, kilns, furnaces and boilers. It helps to produce hundreds of everyday objects, such as bricks, light bulbs, aerosols, cars, paint, clothes and milk bottles.

This factory uses gas flames to make glass bottles.

Liquid gases as fuel

In some rural areas, a **mains gas** supply is not available because it would be too expensive to install. Instead, bottled gas is often used. These are cylinders of LPGs, such as butane and propane. They can be used just like mains gas, for heating and cooking. Perhaps you have used gas cylinders on a camping trip.

Another form of liquid gas is **compressed natural gas (CNG)**. This is used instead of petrol to power cars, lorries and buses.

Bottled gas is ideal for cooking on camping holidays.

It has the advantage of producing very little pollution, and may be cheaper than imported petrol. CNG is used in the USA and New Zealand for example.

This biogas digester in India produces fuel for cooking.

Biogas is another useful form of gas. It can be produced by putting animal manure into a large tank called a digester. Bacteria break the manure down into methane gas, which in turn powers a **generator** to produce electricity. This method of producing gas is often used on farms.

Chemicals from gas

One of the gases contained in natural gas is ethane. Ethane is an example of a gas that is not burned as a fuel to heat or cook with. Instead, it is used to produce such things as **antifreeze**, which is put into car engines in winter.

When ethane is heated in a furnace, a chemical called ethylene is made. Ethylene is used to make all sorts of different plastics. One of these plastics is PVC, which is used in glues and to make raincoats. Another is polystyrene, from which throwaway cups and packaging are made.

Antifreeze prevents engines freezing up in cold weather.

Other plastics products made with chemicals from gas include clear sticky tape, bottles, tool boxes, buckets and hose pipes.

Natural gas is mostly made of methane. Chemicals, such as ammonia, can be made from methane. Ammonia is used to make **fertilizers**, for use on farms.

These plastic raincoats were made using chemicals from gas.

Gas safety

Special 'sniffing' equipment is used to check for leaking gas pipes.

Have you ever wondered why gas smells before it is lit? In fact, natural gas is odourless. The smell is added at the gas refinery before it is sent into people's homes. The gas is checked by experts called rhino-analysts. They have been specially trained to use their noses to sniff the gas to make sure it smells as it should.

The smell is important for safety reasons. Gas burns very easily. Leaking gas could suddenly explode, which would be very dangerous. The smell helps us to recognize when gas is leaking so the supply can be turned off.

This 'sniffer' van can detect gas leaks as it travels along the road.

Gas companies continually check for gas leaks. 'Sniffer vans' drive round at night using special equipment attached to the underside of the van to detect leaks from the mains supply. Many factories and gas rigs have permanent gas alarms installed to warn them of gas leaks.

Fire-fighters and rescuers in France at a collapsed building after a gas explosion.

Gas and the environment

A lot of gas is wastefully burnt off at oil wells.

Natural gas does not cause any visible pollution such as dust, smoke or ash. Nor does it have any wasteful **by-products**. However, gas does contain small amounts of chemicals that get into rain-water and make the water droplets acid. This is called **acid rain**.

When gas is produced, some of the gas is burned off and wasted. This is because it is too expensive to transport it to where it is needed. This is called 'flaring'.

When fossil fuels such as coal, oil or gas are burned, they produce fumes that go into the air. This pollutes the air and makes the earth warmer. It is called the **greenhouse effect**.

However, gas produces less pollution than coal, and today, many power stations that once burned coal are switching to gas instead.

Gas refineries and gas rigs are often ugly to look at. Today gas companies think about this when they are planning new sites to build on. They are keen to look after the natural habitat of a region. Gas pipelines can also cause ugly scars on the landscape. But today, most of them can be buried underground so people do not know that they are there.

Left *A gas pipeline is laid through the countryside.*

Below *By burying the pipeline, the countryside is left unscarred.*

Gas in the future

All the latest technology is used to locate new gas fields.

Russian scientists suggest that enough gas may be found under the Arctic ice-cap to last 30,000 years. However, the known supplies will only last another sixty years. Geologists will probably discover more gas reserves as time goes by, but we should all be trying to conserve our gas supplies as much as possible.

As supplies run short, then prices will rise. This may make it worthwhile to use the gas that is now being wastefully burned off at oil wells.

Large reserves of gas may be discovered under the Arctic ice-cap.

Substitute natural gas (SNG) can be made from coal or oil. This costs more to produce than natural gas, and is not widely used at the moment. However, if natural gas starts to run out, then SNG could replace it since there is enough coal in the world to last a very long time. It may even be possible to convert the coal to SNG without even having to dig it up. This would benefit the **environment**.

The search for new gas fields continues as our known supplies of gas start to run out.

Projects about gas

Warning

Gas must be treated with care. While natural gas is not poisonous, it can easily catch fire or explode.

You should never try and experiment with gas from a cooker or gas bottle.

Air is a gas

The air we breathe in is a mixture of gases – mostly oxygen and nitrogen. Here are some projects for you to try with air.

You will need:

Newspaper   Scissors

1. Cut out two pieces of newspaper about 10 cm sq. Crumple up one sheet into a ball.

2. Hold the crumpled sheet and the uncrumpled sheet in front of you. Drop them both to the ground.

   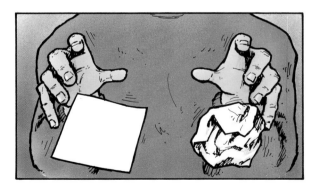

Which piece of paper reached the ground first?

Why did one sheet of paper fall more slowly than the other?

What would happen if you did the same experiment in a vacuum (a place where there is no air)?

28

Does a candle need air to burn?

You will need:

A glass jar
A short candle

Matches to light the candle
A piece of card

1. Ask an adult to help you stick the candle to the piece of card. Light the wick of the candle.

2. Cover the burning candle with the glass jar, and watch what happens.

 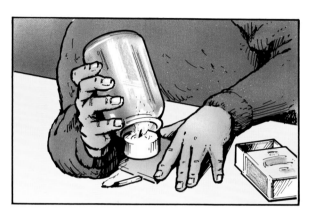

What gas in the air makes the candle burn?

Safety with gas

Here are some of the things that you should and should not do when you smell gas in your home:

Do open doors and windows to get rid of the gas smell.

Do turn off the gas supply at the meter.

Do check the gas has not been left on unlit or that a pilot light is out.

Do phone the gas people.

Do not strike any matches.

Do not turn electrical switches on or off.

Glossary

Acid rain   Rain that has absorbed pollution in the atmosphere and become more acid.

Antifreeze   A chemical that stops car engines freezing up.

By-product   Something that results from a manufacturing process. Often, the by-product is waste.

Central heating   A system for heating the rooms of a building by means of radiators or hot air connected to a source of heat.

Compressed natural gas (CNG) Natural gas that has been 'squeezed' so that it takes up much less space.

Crude oil   Oil before it has been refined.

Cylinder   A hollow container shaped like a tube.

Distribution system   The network of pipes that carries gas to homes and factories.

Drilling rig   The structure that drills a hole into the ground to find gas or oil.

Environment   The surroundings in which animals and plants live.

Exploratory well   A hole bored into the earth to find gas or oil.

Fertilizers   Chemicals put on the soil to help plants to grow.

Generator   A device that makes electricity.

Geologists   People who study the structure of rocks.

Greenhouse effect   The heating up of the earth caused by gases that build up in the atmosphere. These gases allow the heat of the sun in, but slow down its escape.

Impurities   Unwanted materials that have combined with something.

Liquid natural gas (LNG) Natural gas that has been turned to liquid.

Liquid petroleum gases (LPGs) By-products of natural gas that have been turned to liquid and stored in bottles or tanks.

Mains gas   Gas that is distributed by a network of underground pipes.

Offshore   At some distance from the shore.

Plankton   Tiny animals and plants that drift in the sea.

Production   The making of something, often in a factory.

Refineries   Factories for the cleaning of gas or oil.

Refrigerated   Kept cool or frozen.

Satellites   Spacecraft that travel around the earth.

Books to read

Pechley, Roger. **Focus on Gas** (Wayland, 1986)
Sauvain, P. **Oil and Natural Gas** (Macmillan, 1987)
Sauvain, Philip. **Carrying Energy** (Macmillan, 1987)
Twist, Clint. **Fossil Fuels** (Aladdin Books, 1990)

Useful addresses

Australia
Energy Information Centre
139 Flinders Street
Melbourne 3000
Victoria

Canada
Department of Energy, Mines and
    Resources
580 Booth Street
Ottawa, Ontario
M5G 1L5

Energy Resources Conservation
    Board
640-5 Avenue SW
Calgary
Alberta T2P 3G4

New Zealand
Ministry of Energy
PO Box 2337
Wellington
New Zealand

UK
Association for the Conservation of
    Energy
9 Sherlock Mews
London W1M 3RH

British Gas Education Service
PO Box 70
Wetherby
West Yorkshire
LS23 7EA

USA
American Council for an Energy
    Efficient Economy
1001 Connecticut Avenue NW
Washington DC 20036

World Resources Institute
1735 New York Avenue NW
Washington DC 20036

Index

Picture acknowledgements

The publishers would like to thank the following for allowing their photographs to be reproduced in this book: British Gas cover (top), 17, 22 (both), 25 (both); Bruce Coleman Ltd 5 (Dr Frieder Sauer), 8 (Alain Compost); Chris Fairclough Colour Library 20; Natural History Museum 4; Science Photo Library 19 (Prof David Hall) 26, (top, Hank Morgan); Sefton Picture Library cover (bottom), 18; Topham 16 (top), 23; Wayland Picture Library title page, 7, 9, 10, 11, 12, 14 (both), 16 (bottom), 21; Zefa Picture Library 13, 24, 26 (bottom), 27. All illustrations by Brian Davey.